The Prepper's Grid Down Survival Guide

How To Prepare If The Lights Go Out & The Gas, Water Or Electricity Grid Collapses

By Jim Jackson

Disclaimer

This book is intended to be a general guide, to raise awareness, and to help people make informed decisions in the context of their own personal circumstance.

The author accepts no responsibility for any loss or injury be it personal or financial, as a result for the use or misuse of the information in this book. If you have any doubts or concerns after reading this book, please speak to a qualified person before taking any actions.

Contents

Introduction

Chapter 1
Possible Causes Of A Grid Down & The Importance
Of Being Prepared

Chapter 2
When The Grid Collapses (Short Term)

Chapter 3
Preparing For Limited Access Running Water
How To Find It, Purification & Disinfection

Chapter 4
Sanitation
Toilets/Latrines, Hand Washing, Dishes, Bathing &
Trash

Introduction

You have probably experienced a power outage in the past. It wasn't a big deal because you knew it was short-lived. The electric company would have their team working on the problem immediately and you knew you just had to ride out the outage for a bit. You may have even enjoyed the novelty of being completely unplugged. It is very peaceful when the power is out. After about an hour or so, it gets old. You start to get anxious. The kids get bored and you begin to wonder when you will be able to get back to your regularly scheduled life.

Imagine what your life would be like if that power outage extended days, weeks or possibly months. Could you handle it? Are you prepared to live without electricity? If not, you need to do some planning and prepping. This guide will take you through the various scenarios that could leave you in the dark as well as help you prepare to survive the unthinkable— a total grid collapse.

Chapter 1

Possible Causes Of A Grid Down & The Importance Of Being Prepared

If you are still sitting there and thinking, "This could never really happen," consider some of the following scenarios. It is a very real possibility. Those who assume nothing this serious could ever happen in this technological world need to think again. It most certainly can happen. There have been plenty of mini-attacks on the power grid with most being shoved to the bottom of the news feed. Nobody wants to imagine something so horrible happening and the powers that be don't want to incite panic. They do their best to control the information and are quietly working to make the power grids more secure. In the event the grid does go down, government agencies have been practicing and planning on what to do—just in case. Doesn't it make sense that you practice and prepare as well?

*Terrorist attack-Most people assume a terrorist attack involves bombs, planes and armies. Unfortunately, there is more than one way to attack a civilization. For developed countries that rely a great deal on electricity to run  everything in life from our sewer systems to our banks to gas pumps to the way we conduct business, a downed power grid will bring life to a halt. Terrorists have already made several attempts to take down power grids. They are easy targets and wreak havoc on the world as a whole. The attack could be caused by hacking into computer systems or unleashing an EMP (electromagnetic pulse) caused by a nuclear bomb being detonated high up in the atmosphere. The bomb may not do much damage to the earth itself, but the pulse would interrupt the power grid. That would be the ultimate goal.

*Natural disaster-A massive earthquake, strong tornado or other major disaster worked up by Mother Nature can cause a widespread power grid failure. Blackouts have happened in the past, but they have been repaired within days. Imagine if the grid is down for weeks or months. A series of strong storms could immobilize an entire region. Winter snow and ice storms have already been to blame for some pretty serious power failures in the past.

*Solar flares-Solar flares happen pretty often without anybody realizing. However, a major solar flare could create an EMP as mentioned earlier. Back in 1989, a mild solar flare took out the power grid in

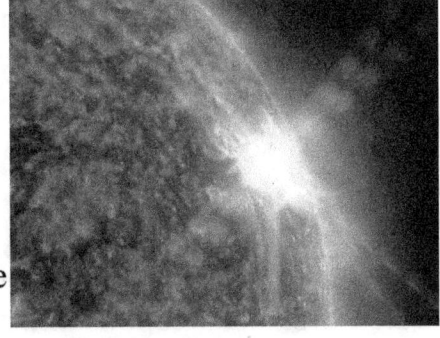

north-eastern Canada. That was nothing compared to what the sun is capable of. The possibility of a major flare could be devastating to the power grid. Scientists have been predicting a major flare is coming for some time.

*__Human failure__-Humans are not perfect. Machinery isn't infallible. There is always the possibility the power grid may fail for no real rhyme or reason. It could take days or months to find the damage and to repair it.

Now that you can understand just how possible it is for the power grid to fail, what are you going to do about it? If you

The Chernobyl disaster of 1986 was a classic example of the tragic consequence of human failure

are smart, you will start preparing to survive the grid failure. Prepping for anything is absolutely crucial to your chances of survival. It is almost impossible to completely imagine life without power. It wouldn't be just your home without power. It would be your neighbourhood, your city, everywhere. You couldn't drive to the next town over to get the supplies you needed. You would be forced to rely on what you had in your home the moment the grid went down.

This is why you want to do your best to prepare a supply of goods that will carry you through a power outage. Food, water, first aid, weapons and survival gear will be necessary to keep you and your family alive. Those who have taken the time to plan and prepare in advance will be the ones who are able to ride out the chaotic aftermath of a failed power grid.

Chapter 2

When The Grid Collapses
(Short Term)

A grid collapse that is short-term means there is light (pun intended) at the end of the tunnel. In the interim, you have to do without. What does that mean exactly? It means the world as you know it comes to a grinding halt. We have become so reliant on electricity, that we are essentially incapacitated without it. Have you ever really thought about how much we depend on electricity?

Check out the things that would be taken or non-existent without power. This is your world without power in the immediate aftermath of a grid failure.

- No access to outside tap water. The water that comes through your tap is cleaned and pumped through with the help of electricity. No electricity means your water supply will become dirty and eventually non-existent. You won't be able to flush your toilet when the water runs out. If you live in a home where you have your own well, you won't have the electricity needed to run your pump, which supplies water to your home.

- No electricity in your home. You will be in the dark. You won't be able to charge your phone, your laptop or your tablet. There is no popping anything into the microwave or cooking on the stove. No refrigeration to keep your food cold and safe to eat. You can't turn on the heater to get warm and you can't turn on the fan to cool down.

- Little or no access to food. You can't run to McDonald's, the grocery store or 7-Eleven to grab something to eat. They don't have power, which means their cash registers don't work. Restaurants won't be able to operate without their grills and other kitchen equipment, which all run on power. There will be no food supply coming in to restock the grocery stores shelves that have been looted or wiped out completely in the aftermath of the grid failure.

- Little or no communication. Most communication systems rely on electricity. Your cell phone may be able to pick up service for a while, but eventually it will go dead. Cordless phones and most other landlines will not work without electricity. Your laptop may be able to connect via Skype or instant messaging for a bit, but that all depends on where the grid failure occurred and if servers are up and running.

- Little or no access to commerce. As mentioned earlier, stores everywhere will be forced to shut down. Without electricity, the registers don't work. The darkness will also prohibit commerce. The lack of electricity will create a state of chaos that will force stores to close their doors in an attempt to preserve their goods. Will it stop looters? No. Doctor's offices, department stores, gas stations and mini-marts will all be closed down, frozen by the lack of power.

- Little to no access to government resources and services. Whether you realize it or not, you depend a great deal on these resources. When the grid goes down, the government will be at a standstill. Police, fire and rescue and local aid agencies are going to have to shut down. Everything relies on computers and without electricity, those computers will be useless. Calling for help in an emergency isn't going to be an option.

- Little or no access to transportation. Whatever gas that is in your car the moment the power grid fails is all the gas you will have. Gas pumps need electricity to run. Without gas, you will be stranded as well as city buses, trucks that haul supplies across the country and even government vehicles like cop cars and ambulances. If an EMP is the source of the power grid failure, it would also knock out the computer systems in your vehicle. Older cars would still be able to run, but without gas, it doesn't matter. Subways and rail systems rely on electricity and would be incapacitated.

- Banking systems will be offline. You can't run to the ATM to draw cash out of your account. The ATMs won't work and the banks will be closed. Without power, the money in the bank will sit there, completely untouchable the legal way. Of course, money isn't going to mean much in a power grid failure because commerce will be at a standstill.

- Nuclear power plants will be at risk of a meltdown. Nuclear power plants require electricity to keep cool. Think back to the disaster in Japan and what that did to the country and the entire world. How many nuclear power plants would be affected by a widespread power grid failure?

These are just some of the most obvious things that will interrupt life as we know it. If you don't realize how much we rely on power, shut off the power to your home and try to go a day without it. You won't be able to have a hot shower in the morning, if you use an electric toothbrush or razor, you are out of luck. You will have to walk to collect water or search for food, but watch out for the thousands of other people that are going to be clogging the sidewalks. When it gets dark, there isn't going to be any street lights or lights from windows to break up the blackness. There will be no hum of electricity overhead or music coming from a building or even a car radio. It is a cold, dark world without electricity. Are you ready?

Chapter 3

Preparing For Limited Access Running Water
How To Find It, Purification & Disinfection

What can you do to prepare for no running water? Plenty! Preparing for limited access to running water today will aid your survival. Water is going to be of utmost importance. Food may feel like it should be a priority, but it really isn't. You can only survive three days without water, but you can survive three weeks without food. Ideally, you would want to store water in case of an event like this or some other disaster that leaves the water supply contaminated or inaccessible. It can be difficult to store more than a couple weeks worth of water so you will need to have a backup plan for replenishing your water.

Each person in your home will need one gallon of water per day for survival. It is extremely difficult to store enough water in your home that will keep your family alive for 30 days or more. In the next section, we will discuss how to find water, but for now, let's focus on what you can do to store some water in the home. Having a case or two of commercially bottled water in the home just makes sense. This ensures you have water for immediate use while you gather your wits and prepare to start finding and hauling water back home.

Depending on the size of your home and where you live i.e. on a large piece of land, in an apartment or in the suburbs, you will have some different options for storing water.

Check out some of the following ways you can store water around your house.

- Cisterns—these are large tanks set above ground on a hill or buried in the ground with a hand pump used to pump water out. The cisterns can hold anywhere from 500 to 1000 gallons of water.
- Swimming pools—kiddie pools are just as good
- Hot tubs
- Man-made ponds with or without fish
- Rain barrels
- Hot water tanks
- Home bottled water—only use plastics that are BPA free and heavy-duty. Old juice bottles and 2-liter pop bottles will work. DO NOT use old milk jugs.

How to Find It

Where do you find the water you need to survive? Depending on where you live, it may be pretty tough. If you have planned ahead, you can map out various sources of water around your home. The goal is not to have to travel more than 5 miles one way. It may not seem like a lot, but carrying several gallons of water back to your home 5 miles is a lot harder than you would think, especially if you have to do that on a daily basis.

Consider all possible sources of water. Ideally, you don't want any water that is downstream from a farm or plant that may have fertilizer run-off or other contaminants. Try and find the water source that is above the farm. Swimming pools, hot tubs, rain barrels and almost any other source is acceptable. However, NEVER drink water before purifying. Pond water is probably something you wouldn't normally consider, but it can be cleaned and purified to become safe for drinking. When drawing the water, fill from the middle of the pond. You don't want to get the sediment on the bottom or the slime on the top.

You will also need to consider how you will transport the water. Have a couple jerry cans on hand—specifically designed to store water. These are blue in colour and look like a gas can. They have handles that makes it easy to carry the water. You may also want to consider making or investing in a cart or wagon you can pull to hold the water.

Stackable water containers with handles are a good idea. The square vessels fit nicely on top of each other and can create a sturdy wall of water. Each jug has a handle and a spout. When the jug is empty, set it aside for transport to your water source. If you don't have any of these items, you can use old water bottles to transport water.

Purification

There are a couple of different ways you can purify water. Purification is different than filtration. Do not get the two confused. A water filter does not remove viruses from the water. Water filters remove impurities, but they should not be used alone if you suspect the water you have may be contaminated. Bodies of water that animals

Portable Cartridge style fillers like the above are very affordable and will remove most particles from the water

drink out of, walk in and defecate in are likely to have viruses in them. You can't see the viruses or smell them, but they are definitely in there. There is no guarantee that water you find will be 100 percent clean and safe to drink. In fact, most purifiers only promise to remove 99.9 percent of viruses and bacteria. That is the best you are going to get.

Chemical Purification

One of the most popular ways of purifying water is with tablets. The tablets may use chlorine or iodine to purify the water. Both methods are effective. However, if a person has a shellfish allergy, they will likely be allergic to the iodine. You can also keep bleach or iodine on hand to use as a purification method. Unfortunately, bleach is only good for about 6 months. You will need to make sure you keep your supply of bleach fresh. Iodine has a longer shelf life as long as it is stored out of direct sunlight and exposure to oxygen.

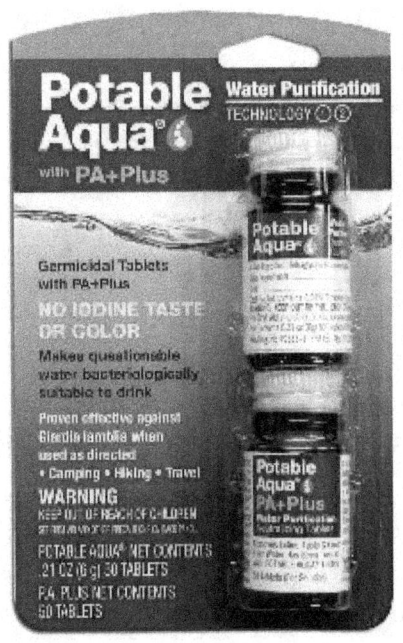

Compact packaged water treatments like this are great as they are easy to store and will eliminate any error when treating water chemically

To purify a gallon of dirty water, you only need about 8 drops of bleach. If the water is especially dirty, you can add up to 16 drops of bleach. A single gallon of bleach can last about a month. Iodine is sold in much smaller bottles and takes much more to purify a single gallon of water. You will need 20 drops of iodine for fairly clear water and 40 drops for cloudy water.

Disinfection

Disinfecting water is very similar to purifying water. There are many different ways to go about doing this. Boiling water is one of the most popular ways. However, when you don't have electricity, this can be a bit of a problem unless you have a proper vessel to use over an open fire. There is another option, calcium hypochlorite. Many

Boiling water is a popular and effective way to kill bacteria BUT this not always viable where gas or electricity is not available and can really deplete your emergency wood, kerosene or propane supplies

survivalists and experienced preppers feel calcium hypochlorite is better than bleach or other purification methods. A single teaspoon can disinfect two gallons of water. This is a very economical way to disinfect water. You can buy a 1-pound bag of the calcium hypochlorite in the swimming pool section of a department store for just a few dollars. It will also store for long periods of time, which makes it more desirable than household bleach. Keep in mind; more is not better. Too much calcium hypochlorite is dangerous and can make you ill.

Filtration can help make water taste a little better and if you are in a desperate situation, a filter will work. There are numerous sizes and styles of water filters. Portable filters are great if you need to bug out to a different location. There are solar-powered filters that you can set up at home. This allows you to have a steady supply of clean water on hand. If you are getting your water from a source that is filled with debris, a filter combined with a chemical purification method is ideal.

Chapter 4

Sanitation
Toilets/Latrines, Hand Washing, Dishes, Bathing & Trash

When the power goes out, the sanitation systems will not be functional. You don't realize what you have until it is gone. A quick trip to the bathroom is a luxury that will be lost when the power grid fails. Everything you know today is going to change the second the grid collapses. To help you understand what you are dealing with, consider the following list of tasks and luxuries that will become major problems without power.

- Toilets/Latrines
- Hand washing
- Dishes
- Bathing
- Trash

How will you handle each of these situations? You need to do some planning so you can handle each of these extremely important tasks. With proper planning, it is completely possible to maintain good sanitation even without electricity.

Toilets-You can approach the toilet situation in a number of different ways.

Outhouse—if you live on your own land, you can take care of this today. If you don't want an outhouse on the property today, you can plan to build one when it is needed. You don't have to have walls, per se, but privacy is going to be appreciated. Digging a hole and placing a bucket or other "seat" over the hole will work for a toilet. You will want to fill in the hole once it is close to being full. Place rocks over the dirt to prevent animals from getting curious. Your latrine should not be near any bodies of water.

You can use a 5-gallon bucket in the house lined with a heavy-ply garbage bag. Put the lid on the bucket when not in use to reduce smell. Change the bag every day or when close to being full.

If water isn't an issue, you can use your toilet and manually flush it with a gallon of water. You can also line the toilet with one of the thick garbage bags. Stock up on kitty litter and place a scoop of litter in each new bag to help absorb the urine and smell.

Handwashing-You absolutely must practice good handwashing to avoid spreading any more germs than necessary. After using the bathroom, digging in the dirt or tending wounds, you must wash your hands thoroughly. Some people suggest setting out a large bowl filled with water for each family member to dip their hands into and wash. While this can work, it isn't ideal. You are washing your dirty hands in the same bowl and expecting them to come out clean.

Ideally, you would want to use a ladle or spoon that would keep your hands out of the water. You could also use a pitcher or jug of water left near your makeshift handwashing station. Use potable water to wash your hands. Drip some of the water over the hands and then add soap. Work the soap in for about 30 seconds making sure to scrub under than nails and up the wrists. Use another scoop of water to rinse the soap off. Warm water is going to be pretty tough to come by, so room temperature water is the best you are going to get. Have a supply of hand sanitizer to use in between washings to keep your hands as clean as possible.

Dishes-You will need to use disinfected water to wash your dishes. Using dirty or contaminated water could make you sick when you eat off the contaminated dishes. Wash dishes as you normally would if you didn't have a dishwasher. Scrape any leftover food away, rinse the dishes, place in soapy water and then rinse again. Allow dishes to air dry.

Bathing-The CDC advises you to use purified water to bathe with. You will likely be relegated to sponge baths unless you have a way to purify a great deal of water to fill up the bathtub. Showering isn't really an option. Remember, the bathwater will be tepid, unless you have a way to heat the water before pouring it in. Bathing is important, but it isn't necessary to take a bath every single day, especially if water is limited. Do your best to get the most important areas to prevent rashes, i.e. under the arms, groin area and feet. This will also cut down on offensive body odour.

Trash-Trash is always going to be an issue. Stock up on heavy-duty garbage bags. Remove the trash from your home regularly to avoid decay, maggots, flies and a whole host of other potentially dangerous conditions that arise from trash building up. Place the trash away from your home. Do NOT place trash near a body of water. You don't want your trash contaminating your water supply.

You will also want to get creative with your trash disposal. Recycling takes on a whole new meaning. You are going to want to do your best to limit the amount of trash you produce. Reuse containers. Tin cans can be rinsed out and used to heat water. Kitchen waste, paper and cardboard can be put into a compost heap. This is one way to use your trash to make your garden grow. Take the time to learn how and what to compost today.

You can burn trash as well. Avoid burning plastics and any containers that held chemicals. Your last option is to bury the trash. Make sure you bury the trash at least 100-feet away from any bodies of water. Dig the hole deep enough that you will have at least 18 inches of dirt on top of the trash. You don't want animals to dig up the trash and spread it around.

Chapter 5

Cooking, Cooling, Lighting & Heating

You need to stay warm or cold, depending on your environment. You only have three hours before your core body temperature becomes an issue. If you are too hot or too cold for more than three hours, you are at risk for hypothermia or hyperthermia. Both conditions can be life-threatening. You need to start thinking about how you will keep your family cool or warm. Another issue will be cooking. How will you heat your canned food or cook meat you have harvested from the wild? Lighting is yet another concern. You need to have some light. You don't need to light up every single room in the house, but you will need light to safely walk to the bathroom, check on family members and to feel safer in general.

Let's start with heating. Basically, your only option is going to be fire. If you have a fireplace in your home, you are set. You only need to worry about having enough firewood on hand or a means to get more. An axe and chainsaw will be important tools to have on hand. Don't wait until the grid fails to try and track one

A simple wood heater like this is a great investment as it can be a great way to save money on gas or electricity if the grid works well BUT if the grid does go down it can be used to heat your home and with a little improvisation can be used to cook with and boil drinking water

down. If you don't have a woodstove or fireplace, it would be a really good idea to get one installed today. Never attempt to use a propane stove in the house to get warm. There is a serious risk of carbon monoxide poisoning.

Cooling is just as important as heating. Although you won't need fans and you will still be slightly warm, you can stay safe by keeping the blinds and curtains closed in your home to block the sunlight. Open windows at night to allow the cool air in, but shut them as soon as the temperatures start to rise in the day. Do your best to keep the door closed to trap as much of the cool air in as possible. If you have a basement, spend the days below ground. These are naturally cooler.

Cooking without electricity is one of your easiest tasks. There are a number of different ways to go about this. Your old Coleman grill will work great—as long as you have fuel. Depending on the severity of the collapsed power grid, you may run out of fuel at some point. You can cook over an open fire, but you need to plan ahead for this by having the proper dishes available. Cast iron cookware is your best option. Solar ovens are easy to make with some tinfoil and a cardboard box. These will only work if you have plenty of unfiltered

Vintage wood stoves like this were designed when there was no grid so they can not only heat your home and cook your food but some of them also feature wet backs which can provide you with a constant supply of hot water

sunlight. You can also buy solar ovens that are very effective and can even be used during the winter months as long as there is a steady stream of sunlight. If you are using a woodstove for heat in your home, you can heat water for coffee or rehydrating your freeze-dried meals. Frying an egg or warming up a can of chilli is also very doable.

Lighting may not seem like a big deal, but it is important to your state of mind. If you are holed up in your home with the windows covered, you will become depressed. Depression isn't something you need to be dealing with at a time when the world has been turned upside down. If you have young children, they will also be comforted by light. There are plenty of options for lighting.

- Solar lights that you normally put outside in your landscaping can be brought inside. This provides plenty of light for the home. It is also an inexpensive option. Place the lights outside during the day to be recharged.

Solar-powered garden lights can be used with great effect for indoor lighting as they are affordable, present no fire hazard and require no fuel or batteries to operate

- Solar-powered lanterns provide a great deal of light as well. They typically have different settings that allow you to have a little or a lot of light.

22

- Candles are an option, but make sure you stock up on emergency candles. Those pretty scented candles don't put off much light. Emergency candles are designed to burn brighter and longer. Make sure you have candleholders and a good supply of matches.

- Flashlights are great for walking outside to use the outhouse, but because batteries are going to be in short supply, this isn't going to be an ideal option for inside the home. If possible, choose LED flashlights. They are brighter and require less battery power.

- Battery-powered touch lights can act as a nightlight. These do tend to burn through batteries pretty quick, so you will want to have a good supply on hand.

How to Maintain a Healthy Environment

Your biggest challenge in a downed grid situation is maintaining a healthy environment. This applies to not only the physical aspect, but the mental aspect as well. Our grandparents would do just fine sitting in a quiet room with little light and their knitting or simply enjoying the peace and quiet. Unfortunately, our children and even some of us have been raised with a constant stream of outside stimuli from bright, flashing lights, televisions, computers, iPods and gaming systems. We have become accustom to constantly being plugged in. There will be a bit of a withdrawal as you and your family learn to cope with being unplugged.

It will also take some adjusting to cook and clean without electricity. Washing clothes, washing dishes and even cleaning the floors has all become reliant upon electricity. It is going to take some practice to learn how to do these things without the benefit of electricity. It is a good idea to get familiar with your options. Have a manual clothes washer on hand. You don't have to use it today, but learn how to just in case. Have a drying rack for the dishes, even if you have a dishwasher. Housework will actually help maintain some sense of normalcy as well as ensure you are doing your best to present the spread of disease and infection.

Stock up on some things to stay occupied when the grid goes down. Believe it or not, there are plenty of forms of entertainment that do not require electricity. You want the items to be relatively new so they are more exciting when you break them out. Stock up on some of the things from the list below to bust out when the lights go out.

- Books
- Magazine
- Jigsaw puzzles
- Crossword puzzles
- Colour crayons and colouring books
- Art supplies
- Board games
- Cards
- Non-electric musical instruments
- Knitting, sewing and other hobbies

If your child has a favourite toy or special blanket, make sure you have it with you. This provides a great deal of comfort in an uncertain time. The idea is to make your home as comfortable as possible. It can be done with a little planning and a positive attitude.

Chapter 6

How to Prepare Now For A Situation Where There Is Little Or No Immediate Access To Food In A Grid Down

Taking the time to plan for a complete breakdown in the food supply chain is crucial. What you have in your kitchen cupboards when the power goes out is likely all you will have until order can be restored. That can take days, weeks or even months. An extensive power outage can cause a severe interruption in the food chain. Grocery stores will be unable to receive shipments due to a lack of transportation. Farmers will struggle to water their crops or even harvest them without machinery.

You have to build up a food supply that will sustain your family. Ideally, you should shoot for a goal of 30 days of food stored in your home or a second location. The government recommends 3 days, but this won't do much in a serious failure of the power grid. Planning for 30 days is adequate, but you will want to continue to build that number up to three months and ultimately one year.

You don't need to run out and buy out the stores and max out your credit cards. This is a process that should be slowly built up over time. Look for sales and stock up when items are discounted. Buying in bulk is often a great way to save money on the food you need. Budget at least $20 a month to your food storage. When you go grocery shopping throw in an extra can of veggies or a box of pasta to add to your storage. Adding a little at a time lessens the impact on your monthly finances.

There are some key foods you will want to include in your food storage. Because water is going to be short, it is a good idea to stay away from foods that are high in salt. Salty foods make you thirsty. You can't afford that. You will also want to choose foods that don't require a lot of water to reconstitute or cook.

Some of the most common survival foods are freeze-dried. There are several reasons why people who are stocking up on food and water for an emergency choose freeze-dried products.

- Require very little water to make edible
- Have higher nutritional value than dehydrated foods
- Large variety of foods available
- Lightweight and easy to carry

Dehydrated foods are an option, but should be kept to a minimum. Canned foods and dried foods are very good items to have in your food storage. The following list includes some of the key foods you will want to store in case of a power grid failure.

- Dried beans; navy, red, pinto
- Grains; flour, wheat
- Canned foods; chilli, ravioli
- Canned meats; tuna, chicken, spam
- Canned fruits and vegetables

- Freeze-dried foods—large variety
- Dried dairy products; butter, instant milk, cheese
- Pasta
- Ramen noodles
- Peanut butter

Those are some basic foods that can help get you by. However, there are a few more things you will want to have on hand to make life a little easier and enjoyable.

- Salt and pepper
- Dried spices
- Chocolate
- Coffee/tea
- Cooking oil
- Alcohol

Many of these items will make great bartering tools. You have to imagine a world where credit cards won't work and ATMs are out of order. Whatever cash is in your wallet when the grid fails is all you will have. You may discover you need something whether it is a few rolls of toilet paper or a propane tank for your barbecue. If somebody has what you need and you have something they need, you can trade or barter.

Do your best to create an adequate food storage that will keep your family healthy and happy for the weeks of living in the darkness. Many of the freeze-dried foods boast shelf lives that can be as long as 25 years. While this is true to some extent, it is important you choose a place to store your food carefully in order to maximize shelf lives. Of course, there are plenty of people who will tell you a best if used by date is more of a guideline and not an actual date set in stone. You can help extend the use by dates by storing your food in an ideal setting. The following criteria should be looked for when you are looking for somewhere in your home to keep your food supply.

- Out of direct sunlight
- No extreme temperatures—ideally below 80 degrees Fahrenheit and above 50 degrees
- Plenty of ventilation
- Dry—no damp walls or floors

It helps to keep your food stores together, but if you don't have a single room or basement available to devote to food storage, make do with what you have. Canned goods and other foods can be stored under the furniture, under the beds, in the back of the closet and throughout the home. Ideally, you will want to keep your stores somewhat out of sight. When darkness prevails, people tend to do things they normally wouldn't. The instinct for survival will create chaos and uncivil behaviour in the most law-abiding citizens. Keeping your food out of sight helps deter people from coming after what you have. Share if you have enough, but advertising your food and water supply is far too risky.

You will also want to get familiar with gardening. You don't have to live on a large plot of land to grow a garden. There are plenty of apartment dwellers who have mastered the art of container gardening. Because your own garden may end up being your only source of food for a while, you will want to stock up on heirloom seeds. Keep these seeds with your food storage. Please note; it has to be heirloom varieties. The typical seed packs you buy in stores are not going to give you renewable seeds. The vegetables produced by those seeds will contain seeds that are not suitable for growing new crops. They will either not sprout or sprout and not produce any vegetables. Spend the extra money and buy a variety of heirloom seeds. When stored correctly, the seeds will last for years. As you harvest your garden, be careful to harvest the seeds to plant more vegetables.

Gardening is a skill that improves with practice. Take the time to learn how to garden today so you are ready when you really need it.

Conclusion

There are always going to be sceptics and those who simply don't believe that a failure of the power grid is possible, but it truly is. Governments are well aware of the risks and are doing what they can to prepare for a massive grid failure. It is only a matter of time before a terrorist gets it right or the sun's solar flares prove too much for our overworked grids. In the past couple of years, there have been numerous "situations" where grids have failed or have been attacked. Computer viruses that are proving to be extremely problematic have also been unleashed on the world. Many believe a single computer virus could be what takes down the grid.

It doesn't really matter what ultimately causes the power grid to fail. What matters is how the citizens prepare and respond. We can live without power. Our ancestors did it for centuries. Unfortunately, our generation is simply not accustomed to doing so and would struggle and possibly die. It is all about preparing for the worst and hoping for the best. Don't let a collapsed power grid risk your life. Spend time learning how you can live without power.

Good luck to you and your family!

From The Author

Thank you for taking the time to read this book. As an author, I understand the importance of creating books which my readers will find both enjoyable and informative. If you have the time and feel generous, please don't hesitate to leave an honest review of this book.........Jim Jackson

Other Books By Jim Jackson

Prepper's Pantry

Are you prepared in the event of an emergency? Do you have ample food storage to keep your family fed during a disaster? If not, then this book will guide you through the process of preparing for anything. These first steps in preparing your pantry will give you peace of mind knowing that you did what was necessary to care for your family. In this easy-to-read guide you will find information and facts you may have never considered and will gather valuable resources to sustain your family. The Prepper's Pantry can be the starting point for making sure your family can survive.

Camping And Cooking For Beginners

Everyone has a camping disaster story and rarely do they have anything to do with wild animals. From forgetting the food to discovering the tent is too small—a myriad of things can go wrong, but with Camping And Cooking For Beginners, your problems are solved. Beginning with the basics, this handy helper starts with a checklist of what you need for your trip. Choosing the right tent, the right sleeping bag and how to start fires without matches (and he's not talking about rubbing two sticks together!) are only a few chapters in the book. The best advice is the authors Top Ten Mistakes First Time Campers Make (and how to avoid them!)—it is invaluable. Get your copy today, before your camping trip and transform your camping experience into the best memory ever!

The Death Of Money

Surviving an economic collapse requires that you be prepared. This small guide will enable you to formulate a plan, allowing you to be proactive instead of reactive to a catastrophic financial crisis. In four chapters, you will gain invaluable knowledge and insight into what it takes to ensure you and your family have the tools necessary to survive the devastating impact of the loss of paper assets. Discover the skills you need to withstand the perils of a vulnerable financial system.

Motorhome Living For Beginners

When you want to change your lifestyle entirely, you need to have enough motivation but you also need to have knowledge about the lifestyle that you are adopting. Many people who want to live in an RV full-time fail to find a balance in their lives which make that living pleasurable, while others can live the dream and learn to compromise on comforts for the sake of freedom. They wake up in the mornings to feel that they have breathed fresh air. They see different scenery every morning if they so wish.

What you need to know before joining them is whether you're cut out for the lifestyle and what differences there are between living in a conventional home and living in an RV. This book bridges that gap in your knowledge, and although you may choose to save a fortune by staying at home, you may also choose the lesser traveled road and discover the benefits of living in an RV.

Both lifestyles, either in an RV or a home, have their pros and cons. Many who choose the RV lifestyle find that adapting their lives comes naturally. It takes a unique and free spirited person to compromise on the luxuries of home living in favor of the adventurous lifestyle offered by RV living, though many do. Once you weigh the pros and cons, you can make the choice wisely, and that's what this book is all about. The book will appeal to the free spirited who seek something more than merely surviving month to month oppressed by mortgage payments and housing taxes.

Both have benefits, though those who live the life they choose, rather than the life chosen for them by responsibility, find that RV life tests their personal boundaries and skills freeing up their lives to live beyond the grid. Journey with us and learn if living in an RV will suit you, and be prepared for the journey of your life.

www.ingramcontent.com/pod-product-compliance
Lightning Source LLC
Chambersburg PA
CBHW070513290526
45790CB00003B/1223